Norman Thelwell

thelwell.

Chris Beetles Limited, 10 Ryder Street, St. James's, London SW1Y 6QB   Tel: 01-839 7551

Copyright Chris Beetles Limited 1989
10, Ryder Street, St. James's
London SW1Y 6QB

Photography by Red Apple
Design by Alan Kitching
Typeset in Bell by Chestnut
Printed by Artigraf

ISBN 1 871136 07 5

Cover
COUNTRY SPORTING LIFE
Signed
Watercolour with pen and ink and bodycolour
$8^{1}/_{2}$ x $12^{1}/_{8}$ inches
Design for Sporting Prints

Back cover
MALLARDS RISING
Signed
Watercolour with bodycolour
$7^{3}/_{8}$ x 11 inches

NORMAN THELWELL

"The things that happen to them happen to ordinary people." Thelwell has over the years produced cartoons of comedy and comment that reflect some part of everyone's lives and the humorous situations they have encountered. In turn he readily accepts that he has been lucky to have made a living out of entertaining such a wide public with his pictures.

Perhaps it was Thelwell's upbringing in the industrial north-west of England in the 1920s-30s that gave his sense of proportion and the opportunity to observe all aspects of life in town and country. Born on 3 May 1923, Norman Thelwell remembers always wanting to draw as a child although throughout his school career art was considered a second-rate subject. He recalls finding drawing and painting much easier than other subjects, "…with drawing the answer was always there in front of you – you only had to look." His childhood anecdotes and remininscences are reflected in the children he has continued to portray in his cartoons. Although he grew up in the industrial area around Birkenhead, images from the countryside were not unknown: draught horses were still widely used, especially on the docks, and there were herds of cattle along the Old Chester Road.

Weekend excursions and holidays on a North Wales farm are recalled in Thelwell's autobiography, *Wrestling with a Pencil,* with a sensitivity and abiding passion for the countryside that has only strengthened throughout his life. There are particularly fond memories of trips to Raby Mere and Dibbensdale, and since that time he has always been captivated by the life and activity of stretches of water. Leaving school in 1939, he joined an office as a junior clerk because at that time, he muses, "…for a boy from a northern industrial town to ask to be an illustrator was like asking to be a ballet dancer!"

In his diaries during the Blitz on Liverpool Thelwell demonstrates, as early as 1941, the ability to recall the mundane with the extraordinary and devastating: "Went to Eddy's farm this afternoon to draw in the stable but we spent most of the time picking up shrapnel and incendiaries in the fields." (1) His call-up papers came in 1941; through the years that followed both in Britain, and then in India, he always travelled with sketchbooks. The urgency of time taught him a great deal and he remembers that "…humans – but mostly in uniform – surged about me everywhere and I found a new compulsion to record turmoil and movement." (2) The first cartoon Thelwell ever had reproduced was an Indian subject for the *London Opinion.*

Government offers to help ex-servicemen continue their education led Thelwell to take up studies at Liverpool College of Art (1947-50). Although attempts at humourous art were subdued in art college classes, memories of the Common Room ringing with laughter and music were an outlet and breeding ground for ideas and comic observations. It was while at college that he married and in 1950 Thelwell, his wife and baby son moved to Wolverhampton where he had taken up a teaching post at the College of Art. His first experience in teaching had left him sadly disillusioned in dealing with those at the infant or 'warrior' stage; it had also left him daubed with paint and shell-shocked! Thelwell realised that children are often oblivious to the rules that govern adult society and the children that he has drawn obviously think the same way.

Thelwell had been teaching for 2 years when he sent his first cartoon in to *Punch* magazine. While working for *Punch* over the next 25 years sixty covers and fifteen hundred illustrations were produced. Regular work for this publication brought him the achievement from which to develop and also propel his pictures out to a wider public. Thelwell explains that "…when I was working for *Punch,* it was very different from working for a newspaper. You had to look at what was happening around you in the world. For example when picture windows in houses were the 'thing', even though people didn't always have a picture to look at!" He had pointed to a fashion in a way that exposed all that was funny and foolish in this suburban need to impress and conform.

By 1956 such was the load of freelance work for *Punch, News Chronicle* and other publications that Thelwell made the decision to leave teaching and take up illustration full-time. It left the family free to move where they liked in the country providing transport to London was available for the artwork. An idea for the daily papers had to be on the drawing board by about 11 a.m. and on the afternoon train by 3 p.m. Thelwell soon discovered that sending in three versions of a cartoon was fatal, as too much choice created too many decisions amongst editorial staff as to the funniest. Any ideas about life as a humorous illustrator being a bundle of laughs must be dispelled; as Thelwell points out, it is hardly a '9-5 job' and he often worked through to the small hours of the morning to finish a drawing. The next three years were spent frustratingly house-hunting. The book *A Place of Your Own* came about from talking to a friend who had encountered the colourful imagination characteristic of house agents and the hair-raising problems that occur. The enlarged version *This Desirable Plot – a dream house-hunters nightmare'* came 10 years later.

The area around Romsey and the Test river valley was familiar to Thelwell from his early days in the army, and a seemingly unmarketable house in Braishfield became the first of several properties taken on by the Thelwells that was 'in need of some modernisation' or 'affording fascinating possibilities.' As the developers took hold throughout the 1960s, so Thelwell became more concerned with the restorations and conservation of Cherry Hill and the two dilapidated cottages on the property. Demolition orders placed upon the two cottages prompted the Thelwells, who had finished work on the main house by then, to restore and rebuild the cottages as one. Finally they leased out Cherry Hill and moved into Amberley, as they had called the cottage.

Although inundated with work and the involvement with the property at Braishfield at the time, they followed up an advertisement for a Cornish watermill. They set off in the car, down along the narrow lanes of the south-west and offered to purchase Penruin Mill the same day. Recounted in his book *A Millstone Round My Neck* is the story of the restoration of Penruin. Fond memories and many fine black and white drawings, sketches and watercolours are a result of the weekends spent there; the sketching and fishing breaks with the family and variety of companions in often uncomfortable conditions as work got slowly underway. His ambitions to be near running water seemed fulfilled – it is a story of deluges of rain lasting days, flooded rivers, lethal plumbing and the successful running of the mill wheel.

Braishfield was left behind at the appropriate time and Penruin was sold when trips to Cornwall were no longer viable. Of Penruin he writes, "There is enormous satisfaction in making something beautiful or restoring something which was once so, particularly when it is likely to give pleasure for 100 years…" (3). The move to Herons Mead in 1968 gave ample scope for an ever-busy mind and for someone who was always setting himself new projects. Herons Mead was a run-down farm cottage with frontage to the River Test and for the first ten years major projects were constantly in process: there were trees to be planted and the water area extended. The ducks, geese, swans and bantams that have inhabited, and at times infested, Herons Mead over the years along with the dogs and his daughter Penelope's pony, only add to the everyday problems of creating one's own lakeside.

The genius of great illustrators and artists is that their ideas are so prolific, imaginative and unique. Thelwell recalls, however, that in the publishing world a new idea would only be yours for a short time; he remembers noticing changes in people's attitudes or dress only to find it soon picked up by other illustrators. The overwhelming success and continuous publication of his books both here and abroad are evidence of the appeal of this most 'English' of illustrators. They have even been translated into languages as far apart as Finnish and Japanese. Thelwell discovered that seriously relayed information can easily appear pompous and pedantic. His books are written as fairly sensible instructions on, for instance, sailing – knowledge he gained from the shipyards at Birkenhead – but the drawings often portray the catastrophic. Caption and cartoon complement one another perfectly.

His delight in the minute details of everyday life are overlooked or unconsidered by the majority of us. They are all the more amusing when portrayed in delightfully complex drawings that can appeal to artists and non-artists alike. It was precisely this uniqueness for which he was criticised in the early 1950s when the trend was for "the exclusion of everything that was not intrinsic to the joke, … But humour cannot, thank goodness, be controlled by theories or confined within dogmatic limits; Thelwell's finds its' proper expression 'in the round' – in a recognisable world." (H. F. Ellis – Foreword to *Thelwell Country*.)

"I tended to do the things I enjoy," Thelwell explains, "which tend to be country subjects." The first pony cartoon in 1953 of the blacksmith asking the small child of her pony's shoes, 'Ow do they feel then?' brought more letters from readers than ever before. It was over a year later that he produced another pony cartoon; he explains in his autobiography that "…I loved drawing cows and pigs and chickens too and my liking for horses sprang from the fact that they are beautiful to draw…" (4). He also admits admiration for people who could seemingly handle these often unpredictable animals. Anyone who has ridden as a child can identify in any pony those Thelwellian characteristics so often portrayed – either murderous intent towards their small riders or taking such infinite care of their bouncing precarious loads.

The term 'Thelwell pony' has since passed into the English language although the ponies are actually a small proportion of Thelwell's artistic output. The *Punch* editors became concerned that the success of the 'ponies' would restrict the known range of Thelwell's creativity. It is wrong to associate Thelwell purely with the very caricatured cartoons of Penelope and Kipper serialised in the *Sunday Express*. His observations were alive to the surrounding world and its' issues. Ideas were often developed from something seen and reproduced without a caption in the belief that "You can't explain what you see necessarily." The timing in his pictures is often set to perfection; Thelwell explains that "…it was nice to produce a picture just before or after the climax because it allows the person free range to imagine what may have happened." His pictures furthermore provide almost a social report on the changes in Britain since the last war and Thelwell found himself almost alone amongst the illustrators in regularly depicting aspects of the countryside. Pre-war *Punch* had filled its pages with galloping hooves and smoking guns and there seemed to be only Thelwell who has, since that time, seriously upheld the real traditions of the countryside.

Wider issues are encompassed in the everyday happenings: farmers grumble about the weather and when the time came to join the EEC felt they would also have the European weather to worry over; a very real awareness and concern over our 'effluent society' appeared in cartoons time and again; the conflicting interests of leisure and industry and the rise of battery farming. "I can think what I like," he states, "but I believe that I helped to start the anti-battery farming movement in Britain."

Thelwell believes that, because he never attacks with a 'full-frontal' in his pictures, he is more successful in getting the message over; an oblique observation given several times has a longer lasting effect and means the artist gives himself more room to manoeuvre – either to enforce or soften if the theme is taken up once more. Often unpleasant traits and characteristics are shown in his people, but in such a way that we can laugh or sympathize with them: everyone has been through a fraught or frustrating situation only to find it amusing when seen after some time. Another secret to his success is that his people are individuals but not particular ones, we all know them as collective groups in society. There is the good neighbour who will still throw the rubbish over the garden fence when you are not looking, the holiday-makers' almost uncontrollable instinct to form queues to resorts or flocks on beaches, and in the 1950-60s the destruction of beauty spots or old buildings for a so-called better world. All in all what Thelwell terms as "the endearing lunacy of human behaviour." (5). Thelwell continues to draw the world around him with the same enthusiasm he has shown since childhood, his particular love remaining his beloved England and the wildlife that is at home here.

In an 'Artists Profile' article in *Punch* of July 7 1965 Patrick Skene Catling explains of the early illustrators' traditions: "For all their dissimilarities, for all the stylistic peculiarities of their own and of their periods, they shared the orthodox English artistitic virtues, a pragmatic sense of public decency, a clear eye, a steady, workmanlike hand and a warm, even sentimental heart." Included in the forefront of this tradition is Norman Thelwell.

Jacqui Grossart

© Chris Beetles Limited

Notes
1. *Wrestling with a Pencil*, by Norman Thelwell, page 36; published by Methuen London Ltd., 1986
2. *Wrestling with a Pencil*, page 43
3. *A Millstone Round My Neck*, by Norman Thelwell, page 174; published by Eyre Methuen., 1981
4. *Wrestling with a Pencil*, page 91
5. *Wrestling with a Pencil*, page 58

Books by Norman Thelwell

First published	Paperback edition	
1957	1970	*Angels on Horseback*
1959	1970	*Thelwell Country*
1960		*A Place of Your Own*
1961		*Thelwell in Orbit*
1962	1969	*A Leg at Each Corner*
1964	1982	*Top Dog*
1965	1969	*Thelwell's Riding Academy*
1967	1972	*Up the Garden Patch*
1970	1975	*This Desirable Plot*
	1970	*Thelwell's Horsebox (containing A Leg at Each Corner, Thelwell's Riding Academy, Angels on Horseback and Gymkhana paperbacks)*
1971	1982	*The Effluent Society*
1972	1975	*Penelope*
	1972	*Thelwell's Pony Painting Book*
1973	1976	*Three Sheets in the Wind*
1974	1977	*Belt Up*
1975	1982	*Thelwell Goes West*
	1976	*Thelwell's Leisure Chest (containing Up the Garden Patch, The Compleat Tangler, Thelwell's Book of Leisure and This Desirable Plot paperbacks)*
1977	1982	*Thelwell's Brat Race*
1977		*Thelwell Frieze*
1978	1982	*A Plank Bridge by a Pool*
	1978	*Thelwell's Laughter Case (containing The Effluent Society, Belt Up, Three Sheets in the Wind and Top Dog paperbacks)*
1979	1982	*Thelwell's Gymkhana*
1979		*Pony Birthday Book*
1980		*Horse Sense*
1981	1966	*Thelwell's Pony Cavalcade (including Angels on Horseback, A Leg at Each Corner and Thelwell's Riding Academy)*
1981	1983	*A Millstone Round My Neck*
1982	1984	*Some Damn Fool's Signed The Rubens Again*
1983	1985	*Thelwell's Magnificat*
1984		*Thelwell's Sporting Prints*
1986		*Wrestling with a pencil*
1987	1988	*Play It As It Lies*
1988	1989	*Thelwell's Pony Panorama (including Penelope, Thelwell Goes West and Gymkhana)*
1989		*Penelope Rides Again*

Not illustrated in catalogue

149
CHALK PITS IN THE TEST VALLEY
Signed and dated July 18. 1976
Watercolour
10½ x 13¾ inches
Illustrated: *Wrestling with a Pencil*, page 101;
published by Methuen London Ltd., 1986

150
SHEEP FARM IN MID WALES
Signed and dated '75
Watercolour
9⅝ x 14⅛ inches
Illustrated: *Wrestling with a Pencil*, page 151;
published by Methuen London Ltd., 1986

151
POPLARS IN THE TEST VALLEY, HAMPSHIRE
Signed and dated August 15. 1976
Watercolour
10½ x 14⅞ inches

152
ST. ANDREW'S CHURCH, TIMSBURY
Signed
Watercolour with pen and ink and bodycolour
7½ x 11⅜ inches

153
THE LONG, HOT SUMMER OF '76
Signed
Watercolour with crayon
7⅜ x 10⅞ inches

154
SKETCH: HOW TO DRAW PONIES —
ALL THE SECRETS REVEALED BY THELWELL
Signed
Watercolour, pen and ink and pencil
7 x 7½ inches

155
CORFE CASTLE, DORSET
Signed
Watercolour
8¼ x 12⅛ inches

156
WEST COUNTRY RIVER
Signed and dated 1982
Watercolour
16 x 19⅝ inches

157
HAMPSHIRE FARM
Signed and dated 1988
Oil on board
16 x 20 inches

158
INVITATION TO THELWELL EXHIBITION 1965
Pen and ink
9½ x 6½ inches

1
'I'M SORRY I EVER MENTIONED HE'D GOT A STONE IN HIS HOOF.'
Signed and inscribed with title in pencil
Pen and ink
7 1/4 x 6 1/4 inches
Illustrated: 'Angels on Horseback – and Elsewhere', page 50;
published by Methuen & Co. Ltd., 1957

2
'Pretty-pretty'
Signed and inscribed with title in pencil
Pen and ink
8½ x 11¼ inches
Illustrated: Punch, November 3 1952, page 17; *Angels on Horseback – and Elsewhere',* page 93,
published by Methuen & Co. Ltd., 1957

3
JUST LOOK AT IT!. 'LACKS INITIATIVE…EASILY DOMINATED'
Signed and inscribed with title in pencil
Pen and ink
7¼ x 6¼ inches
Illustrated: Punch, June 24 1953, page 747; *'Angels on Horseback – and Elsewhere',* page 82,
published by Methuen & Co. Ltd., 1957

4

'P.S. PLEASE EXCUSE THE SCRIBBLE.'
Signed and inscribed with title in pencil
Pen and ink
8¾ x 11 inches
Illustrated: Punch, July 6 1953, page 13

5

THE COUNTRYSIDE NOMAD
Signed
Pen and ink
6 x 11 inches
Illustrated: Punch, July 6 1953, page 48;
page 84, *'Thelwell Country',*
published by Methuen & Co. Ltd., 1959

6

THE OLD COMBINE HARVESTER
Signed
Pen and ink
7½ x 10½ inches
Illustrated: Punch, August 26 1953, page 263;
'Thelwell Country', page 29,
published by Methuen & Co. Ltd., 1959

7
ANNIE
Signed
Pen and ink
7¾ x 10½ inches
Illustrated: Punch, June 16 1954, page 718

8
THE GYPSY TOURISTS
Signed
Pen and ink
5¼ x 10⅜ inches
Illustrated: Punch, October 13 1954, page 472

9
'I LIKE IT. BUT IS IT NEW?'
Signed and inscribed with title in pencil
Pen and ink with monochrome colour wash
9¼ x 12½ inches
Illustrated: Punch, June 30 1954, page 772

10
WILLOWBROOK SHOW ON THE GREEN
Pen and ink with watercolour
12¼ x 9 inches
Sketch for illustration in Punch, March 9 1955, page 317;
'Angels on Horseback – and Elsewhere'
published by Methuen & Co. Ltd., 1957

BAD LUCK FOR SHIRLEY WILKINSON ON 'TEARAWAY'
WHO HAD A NUMBER OF FAULTS

TOM JENKINS' 'THISTLEDOWN' WAS A POPULAR
ENTRY

FOUR YEAR OLD PENELOPE BRIGHT RIDING 'NIMBLE'
TAKES THE RAILS

'WELL JUMPED MARY!' LAUGHED MRS. HORNBY-SMITH
WHO PRESENTED THE PRIZES

11
COMPLETE HOUSE FURNISHERS
Signed
Pen and ink
7 x 10½ inches
Illustrated: Punch, November 13 1957,
page 568

12
'I SEE YOU'VE KICKED THE TOES OUT OF THEM ALREADY'.
Signed and inscribed in pencil with title
Pen and ink
3⅜ x 5⅜ inches
Illustrated: *Angels on horseback – and Elsewhere*, page 19;
published by Methuen & Co. Ltd., 1957

13
THE HUNT
Pen and ink
8 x 17 inches
Illustrated: *'Angels on Horseback – and Elsewhere'*, pages 80–81;
colour illustration of same subject produced in Punch,
November 1 1954, page 34

14
'HENRY! HENRY! YOU MAD FOOL! LET HIM OVERTAKE'.
Signed and inscribed with title in pencil
Pen and ink with zipatone
5⅛ x 13⅜ inches
Illustrated: News Chronicle, 1958 (when the first stretch of the
new motorway was opened); *'Wrestling with a Pencil'*, page 71,
published by Methuen & Co. Ltd., 1986

15
HELPFUL NEIGHBOURS
Signed
Pen and ink
5¼ x 7½ inches
Illustrated: Punch, August 26 1959,
page 66

16
'.... AND OF COURSE ITS PEOPLE'.
Signed with initial
Pen and ink
6½ x 5¼ inches
Illustrated: Punch, July 16 1958, page 91;
'Thelwell Country', page 96,
published by Methuen & Co. Ltd., 1959
'Wrestling with a Pencil', page 83, published by
Methuen & Co. Ltd., 1986

17
THE GOLF BABY
Signed
Pen and ink
6½ x 6 inches
Illustrated: Punch, September 29 1954, page 404;
'Angels on Horseback – and Eleswhere', page 82,
published by Methuen & Co. Ltd., 1957

18
BAGGED
Signed
Pen and ink
5¾ x 7½ inches
Illustrated: 'Thelwell Country', page 68,
published by Methuen & Co. Ltd., 1959

19
A Bad Day at the Shoot
Signed
Pen and ink
5½ x 7 inches
Illustrated: *'Thelwell Country'*, page 68,
published by Methuen & Co. Ltd., 1959

20
The huntsman and the Hitch-Hiking Tramp
Signed
Pen and ink
5½ x 8 inches
Illustrated: *'Thelwell Country'*, contents page 7,
published by Methuen & Co. Ltd., 1959

21
THELWELL COUNTRY — METHUEN & CO. LTD FRONTISPIECE
Signed
Pen and ink
$10^3/4 \times 8^1/2$ inches
Illustrated: *'Thelwell Country',*
published by Methuen & Co. Ltd., 1959

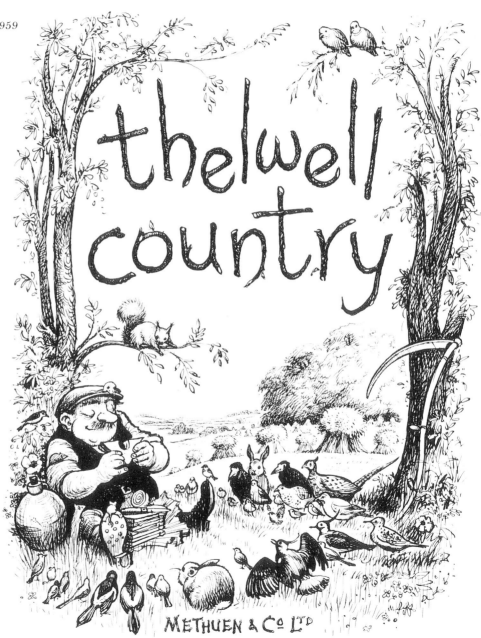

22
THE NEW FOREST PONY: 'DUE TO AN ABUNDANCE OF TRAFFIC IN THE
AREA — THIS RATHER NAROW BREED IS SAID TO BE IMMUNE TO THE
TERROR OF THE MODERN ROADS'.
Signed
Pen and ink
5⅛ x 8 inches
Illustrated: *'Angels on Horseback – and Elsewhere',* page 13,
published by Methuen & Co. Ltd., 1957

23
THE AA MAN AND THE HOLIDAY QUEUES
Signed
Pen and ink
7½ x 10¾ inches
Illustrated: Punch, June 1 1960, page 749

24

'HEY PETE! THERE'S A REAL BEAUTY OVER HERE WITH VITAL
STATISTICS OF TWO AND A HALF, NOTHING AND NINETY-SIX'.
Signed and inscribed in pencil
Pen and ink with zipatone
7 x 11½ inches
Illustrated: News Chronicle 1958, *Wrestling with a Pencil',* page 89,
published by Methuen London Ltd., 1986

25
'WHICH SHALL WE PARCEL UP FOR HIM FOR CHRISTMAS?'
Signed and inscribed with title in pencil
Pen and ink
5¾ x 10¾ inches
Illustrated: Punch, December 7 1960, page 802

26
'Ask Gaffer what's brought 'im to
the verge of ruin this year. The
rain or the drought?'
Signed and inscribed with title
in pencil
Pen and ink with zipatone and crayon
$6\frac{1}{2} \times 10$ inches
Illustrated: News Chronicle

27
'Here comes Charlie! Let's have a
rubber of Bridge'.
Signed and inscribed with title
Pen and ink with zipatone and crayon
$6\frac{1}{8} \times 12\frac{1}{2}$ inches
Illustrated: News Chronicle; *Thelwell
Country'*, page 57,
published by Methuen & Co. Ltd., 1959

28

'Now we mustn't lose our temper, Wendy – perhaps we'll
be good enough for the gymkhana next year',
Pen and ink with zipatone
7½ x 12¾ inches
Illustrated: News Chronicle

29
THE WATER-FOWLER
Signed
Pen and ink
6 x 11½ inches
Illustrated: Punch, February 21 1962, page 319

30
THE BOGGY RUGBY PITCH
Signed
Pen and ink
4⅛ x 10½ inches
Illustrated: Punch, December 27 1961

31
'HE MAKES ME SICK – RUNS A VINTAGE BENTLEY TOO'.
Signed and inscribed with title in pencil
Pen and ink with monochrome colour wash
8¼ x 10¾ inches
Illustrated: Punch, January 24 1962, page 161

'What makes me so mad is being ruined every year by
the weather'.
Pen and ink with zipatone
$6^5/_8$ x $11^7/_8$ inches
Illustrated: News Chronicle

33
'EVER SINCE CHILDHOOD. I'VE NEVER WANTED ANY OTHER
LIFE BUT FARMING'.
Signed and inscribed with title
Pen and ink with monochrome colour wash
6¾ x 10½ inches
Illustrated: Punch, September 6 1961, page 355

34
A SAFETY BELT FOR TWO
Signed
Pen and ink with monochrome colour wash
4 x 10½ inches
Illustrated: Punch, March 21 1962, page 143

35
AMERICAN TOURISTS ARRIVE IN BRITAIN
Signed
Pen and ink with monochrome colour wash
7¼ x 10½ inches
Illustrated: Punch, June 6 1962, page 860

36
'I'd like to see General Charles de Gaulle influence his agricultural policy.'
Signed and inscribed with title in pencil
Pen and ink with monochrome colour wash and crayon
8 x 10½ inches
Illustrated: Punch, January 9 1963, page 66

37

'YOU'RE BOUND TO FEEL NERVOUS
THE FIRST TIME ON TELEVISION.'
Signed and inscribed with title
Pen and ink with monochrome colour wash
6¼ x 10½ inches
Illustrated: Punch, June 5 1963, page 808;
The Effluent Society, page 66,
published by Methuen & Co. Ltd., 1971;
Wrestling with a Pencil, page 92
published by Methuen & Co. Ltd., 1986

38

'PARKINSON, WOULD YOU MIND FILLING
THE WATERING-CAN FROM THE TAP?'
Signed and inscribed with title in
pencil under mount
Pen and ink with monochrome wash
7½ x 10¾ inches
Illustrated: Punch, August 7 1963,
page 199

39
'NO, DON'T TELL ME…'
Signed and inscribed with title
Pen and ink with monochrome colour wash
5¼ x 7½ inches
Illustrated: Punch, August 21 1963, page 275

40
'DON'T YOU EVER RELAX, J.B.?'
Signed and inscribed with title
Pen and ink with monochrome colour wash
7¾ x 11 inches
Illustrated: Punch, September 4 1963, page 334;
'Thelwell's Book of Leisure', page 4,
published by Methuen & Co. Ltd., 1968

41

THE WAR OF THE YEAR:
ALMANACK COLOUR PAGE
Signed
Pen and ink with watercolour
13¼ x 20½ inches
Illustrated: Punch, November 6 1963,
pages 673–4

1. Ten-year-old Nigel, son of Wing-Commander Delamere, British Resident in the oil Protectorate of Djibruli is threatened by natives on his way to school in the Residency car. Delamere seeks protective escort from Brigadier Arbuthnot, o/c British troops in Djibruli, who leads operation in person.

2. Lost in a sudden sandstorm, Arbuthnot leads force over the border into Bauwau, a state hostile to the Sultan of Djibruli and linked to Russia by a treaty of non-aggression. All are captured.

3. Delamere cables London for reinforcements. A combined expeditionary force is mounted without delay.

4. Sultan Gh'ari Potti mobilises, levies armed forces tax, clamps down on imports of Cadillacs from the U.S. Accuses Delamere of plot to reinforce the Bauwauis with British armour in preparation for invasion of Djibruli. Has him arrested.

5. There are repercussions everywhere, as the American motor industry sees trouble ahead.　→

6. The crisis point is nearing. World forces converge.

7. President Kennedy holds a momentous press conference, at which he states his intention of taking all possible steps to avert the imminent upsurge of unemployment in the American auto industry. He appeals to Sheikh Ali Ba Hahma, ruler of Bauwau, to release the British captives and to Sultan Gh'ari Potti to demobilise the Djibruli forces. If they will agree to do so . . .

8. The statesmanlike offer is accepted. World forces disperse.

9. Wing-Commander Delamere and Nigel are reunited.

10. And President Kennedy emerges once more as a Great President, perhaps for the last time.

42
It is important to pick the right breed for your home
Signed
Pen and ink
4¼ x 5¼ inches
Illustrated: *'Top Dog',* page 11;
published by Methuen & Co. Ltd., 1964

43
Don't have a dog that takes over the house
Signed
Pen and ink
3½ x 5¾ inches
Illustrated: *'Top Dog',* page 14;
published by Methuen & Co. Ltd., 1964

44
So if you want a watchdog — make sure you get a good one
Signed
Pen and ink
3¼ x 3½ inches
Illustrated: *'Top Dog',* page 19;
published by Methuen & Co. Ltd., 1964

45

SEE THAT HIS TEETH ARE CLEAN AND WHITE
Signed
Pen and ink
3 x 4 inches
Illustrated: *'Top Dog'*, page 52;
published by Methuen & Co. Ltd., 1964

46

AND HIS NOSE COLD AND DAMP
Signed
Pen and ink
2½ x 3¾ inches
Illustrated: *'Top Dog'*, page 52;
published by Methuen & Co. Ltd., 1964

47

THE SHOW DOG
Signed
Pen and ink
5½ x 4 inches
Illustrated: *'Top Dog'*, page 107;
published by Methuen & Co. Ltd., 1964

48

'TRUST'
Signed
Pen and ink
5¼ x 5½ inches

49
'I'VE GOT A THREE-LITRE ROVER AT THE
MOMENT — ABOUT A MILE OUTSIDE
SALFORD.'
Signed and inscribed with title
Pen and ink
5½ x 8 inches
Illustrated: Punch, August 26 1964,
page 293;
'Thelwell's Book of Leisure', page 13,
published by Methuen & Co.Ltd., 1968

50
THE DOCTORS' VERDICT
Signed
Pen and ink with monochrome colour wash
6 x 9¾ inches
Illustrated: Punch, January 20 1965, page 95

51

THERE IS NO POINT IN BEING WELL-GROOMED YOURSELF
UNLESS YOU ARE PREPARED TO MAKE YOUR PONY...LOOK
THE SAME
Signed and inscribed with title
Pen and ink
11¼ x 4¼ inches
Illustrated: *'Riding Academy',* pages 88-89;
published by Methuen & Co. Ltd., 1965

52

SOME RIDERS FAVOUR A LOT OF BANDAGES ON THEIR HORSE
THIS IS NOT ALWAYS AS POINTLESS...AS IT MAY APPEAR
Signed
Pen and ink
10¼ x 5 inches
Illustrated: *'Riding Academy',* page 83-84;
published by Methuen & Co. Ltd., 1965

53

'Have you finished with the Sunday papers yet?'
Signed and inscribed with title
Pen and ink with monochrome colour wash
7¼ x 7¼ inches
Illustrated: Punch, February 9 1966, page 201

54

'We bought it mainly to cover a damp patch.'
Signed and inscribed with title in pencil
Pen and ink with monochrome colour wash and crayon
4¾ x 11¼ inches
Illustrated: Punch, January 5 1966, page 5

55
CLOSED FOR LUNCH
Signed
Pen and ink with monochrome colour wash
7 x 10³/₈ inches
Illustrated: Punch, January 19 1966, page 78

56
PUNCH COVER: OCTOBER 3RD
Pen and ink
10¾ x 8¼ inches

57
'NEXT'
Signed and inscribed with title
Pen and ink with monochrome colour wash
5¼ x 7 inches
Illustrated: Punch, April 19 1967, page 564

" NEXT "

58
THE OFFICE GOLFER
Signed
Pen and ink with monochrome colour wash
3½ x 10½ inches
Illustrated: Punch, August 2 1967, page 162;

59
'I DIDN'T SPOT THAT POLLUTION 'TILL IT WAS TOO LATE.'
Signed
Pen and ink
6 x 8 inches
Illustrated: Punch, August 9 1967, page 28;
'Thelwell's Book of Leisure',
published by Methuen & Co. Ltd., 1968

60
'A NUMBER FOUR IRON'
Signed and inscribed with title
Pen and ink with monochrome colour wash
4¼ x 10½ inches
Illustrated: Punch, January 29 1969, page 155

61
A PREVIOUS YEAR'S MODEL
Signed
Pen and ink with crayon
6½ x 10¼ inches
Illustrated: Punch, December 6 1967, page 848;
'The Effluent Society', page 31;
published by Methuen & Co. Ltd., 1971

62
THELWELL'S COMPLEAT TANGLER
Signed
Watercolour pen and ink
8½ x 13⅜ inches
Illustrated: Dust Jacket to hardback edition of
'Thelwell's Compleat Tangler'
published by Methuen & Co. Ltd., 1967

63
'I DON'T WANT TO LOAN — I WANT FRIENDSHIP.'
Signed
Pen and ink with monochrome colour wash
6 x 7½ inches
Illustrated: Punch, May 8 1968, page 675

64
THE CURIOSITY SHOP
Signed
Pen and ink with monochrome colour
wash and crayon
6½ x 9¼ inches
Illustrated: *'Thelwell's Book of Leisure'*,
page 10;
published by Methuen & Co. Ltd., 1968

65
'YOU'D BETTER GET WASHED AND
CHANGED. THEY'RE HAVING COMPANY.'
Signed and inscribed with title
Pen and ink with monochrome colour
wash and crayon
6 x 9¾ inches
Illustrated: Punch, 3 June 1970,
page 821;
The Effluent Society', page 80,
published by Methuen & Co. Ltd., 1971;
'Wrestling with a Pencil', page 87,
published by
Methuen & London Ltd., 1986

66
'RUN ALONG AND HELP GRANDAD
FREEZE THE CHICKENS!'
Signed and inscribed with title
Pen and ink with monochrome
colour wash
6¼ x 9½ inches
Illustrated: Punch, July 1 1970,
page 23;
'The Effluent Society', page 41,
published by Methuen & Co. Ltd., 1971;
'Wrestling with a Pencil', page 127,
published by
Methuen & London Ltd., 1986

67
STUDENT DEMONSTRATORS
Signed
Pen and ink with monochrome colour wash
6½ x 9 inches
Illustrated: Punch, July 22 1970, page 134;
'The Effluent Society', page 88;
published by Methuen & Co. Ltd., 1971

68
'I PROMISE YOU THE VERY NEXT DRAMA
SPOT WE GET.'
Signed and inscribed with title
Pen and ink
6¼ x 8¼ inches
Illustrated: Punch, November 18 1970,
page 716

69
THE T.V. ADDICTS
Signed
Pen and ink
7 x 9³⁄₈ inches

70
THE EFFLUENT SOCIETY
Signed
Pen and ink
6 x 10¹⁄₄ inches
Illustrated: Punch, March 17 1971, page 367;
'Wrestling with a Pencil', page 125;
published by Methuen London Ltd., 1986

71
'Hold it Simpson! He's a trusty'
Signed and inscribed with title
Pen and ink
5 x 9¼ inches
Illustrated: *'The Effluent Society'*, page 47;
published by Methuen & Co. Ltd., 1971

72
'I must admit they knew their job.
They left without taking anything.'
Signed and inscribed with title
Pen and ink
7 x 9½ inches
Illustrated: Punch, March 15 1972,
page 366

73
'You little beast — You've been eating Tonto's peppermint cremes.'
Signed with initial
Pen and ink
$4^3/_8$ x $6^1/_2$ inches
Illustrated: Punch, July 25 1973, page 98;
'A God called Horse.'

74
'You know that illegal fence they put across the bridlepath'
Signed with initial and inscribed with title in pencil
Pen and ink
4 x $4^1/_2$ inches
Illustrated: Punch, November 6 1974, page 787;
Oh Didn't he ramble… News that vigilante groups of ramblers are on the warpath to stop the increasing closure of public rights-of-way sent ace war reporter Thelwell sprinting up to the front.'

75
The Champion
Signed
Pen and ink
4 x 3 inches
Illustrated: Punch, July 25 1973, page 99;
'A God called Horse.'

76
'I NEVER TIRE OF LOOKING AT THE SEA'
Signed and inscribed with the title in pencil
Pen and ink
9¼ x 11¼ inches

77
CARRYING THE FLAG
Signed
Pen and ink
7³/₈ x 9³/₄ inches
Illustrated: Punch, July 21 1976, page 112;
'Anne's across the Sea,'; Design used to promote fund-raising
for the British Olympic Equestrian Team 1976.

78
'NO BALL! — HALF A YARD OF DRAG AND THEN YOU
THREW IT.'
Signed and inscribed with title
Pen and ink with monochrome colour wash and crayon
6 x 12 inches

79
ENGLISH SPROUT SELLER — MONTMARTRE
Signed
Pen and ink
7 x 4½ inches

80
'THIS IS THE MOMENT OF TRUTH.'
Signed and inscribed in pencil with title
Pen and ink
6½ x 10 inches

81
PENELOPE AND KIPPER
Signed
Pen and ink
5 x 3½ inches

82
YOU'RE GETTING NO MORE CHOCOLATE, NO MORE PONY NUTS,
NO MORE CAKE... YOU'RE GETTING NOTHING! DO YOU HEAR?
NOTHING! TILL YOU CONVINCE ME THAT YOU DESERVE IT!
Pen and ink
8 x 4¾ inches
Illustrated: Sunday Express; *'Penelope'*,
published by Eyre Methuen Ltd., 1972

83

'SOMETIMES I WONDER HOW ONE CREATURE CAN DOMINATE
ANOTHER CREATURE SO COMPLETELY.'
Pen and ink
2½ x 9 inches
Illustrated: Sunday Express, 1969

83a

'SOMETIMES I WONDER, PENELOPE, WHETHER HORSES
REALLY ARE THE FRIENDS OF MAN.'
Pen and ink
2½ x 9 inches
Illustrated: Sunday Express

84
'WE SHOULD NEVER HAVE GIVEN HER THAT TRUMPET FOR
CHRISTMAS'
Signed and inscribed with title
Pen and ink with pencil
9¾ x 7¾ inches

85
'When I was a kid I had to make do with a push-bike.'
Signed with initial and and inscribed with title in pencil
Pen and ink with monochrome colour wash
2½ x 6 inches

86
See how the vet operates
Signed with initial
Pen and ink
2¾ x 4¼ inches

87
The Zealous Huntsman
Signed
Pen and ink with colour wash
5¼ x 4¾ inches
Illustrated: Lilliput

88
MERRY CHRISTMAS
Pen and ink with colour wash and crayon
$6^5/_8$ x $8^7/_8$ inches

89

USE THE BODY BRUSH VIGOROUSLY — HE WILL ENJOY IT
Signed
Pen and ink
5¾ x 7 inches
Version of an illustration in *'Angels on Horseback'*,
published by Methuen & Co. Ltd., 1957

90

TO ENSURE AGAINST PENALTIES FOR A KNOCK-DOWN
Signed
Pen and ink
9¾ x 7 inches
Illustrated: *'Angels on Horseback'*, page 30-31;
published by Methuen & Co. Ltd., 1957

91
YOU'LL NEED PLENTY OF TIME TO WAKEN YOUR PONY
Signed with initial
Pencil 1 7/8 x 2 1/4 inches

92
SHARING FIRST PRIZE
Signed with initial
Pencil 2 x 2 1/8 inches

93
GAMES FOR FUN
Signed with initial
Pencil 2 x 2 inches

94
PONIES LEARN ANY MANNERS TAUGHT TO THEM
Signed with initial
Pencil 1 3/4 x 2 1/4 inches

95
YOU CAN TAKE THEM TO WATER —
BUT YOU CAN'T MAKE THEM DRINK
Signed with initial
Pencil 2 x 2 inches

96
SMALL THINGS OFTEN
FRIGHTEN PONIES
Signed with initial
Pencil 2 x 2 1/8 inches

97
THE UNBREAKABLE TOY
Signed with initial
Pencil 1 7/8 x 2 1/4 inches

98
THEY CAN FORGET TO BE CAREFUL
OF WHERE THEY PUT THEIR FEET
Signed with initial
Pencil 1 3/4 x 2 inches

99
<small>Insufficient exercise, however, can lead to
excessive fat</small>
Signed with initial
Watercolour, pen and ink
6 x 6 inches
From a sketch in *'Riding Academy',*
published by Methuen & Co. Ltd., 1965

100
Acquiring a pony is not as easy as it sounds
Signed
Pen and ink
8½ x 10¼ inches
Version of illustration in 'A Leg at Each Corner',
published by Methuen & Co. Ltd., 1962

101
PONY CAVALCADE
Signed
Pen and ink with monochrome colour wash
7 x 9½ inches
Sketch for the front cover of 'Pony Cavalcade',
published by Methuen, London 1981

102
THE HAY CART
Signed and dated '79
Watercolour with pen and ink with crayon
8¹/₈ x 11¹/₄ inches

103
THE ORCHARD, HERONS MEAD
Inscribed with title. Pencil sketches on reverse
Pen and ink with pencil and watercolour
$7\frac{1}{8}$ x $9\frac{5}{8}$ inches

104
THE GARDEN ROLLER AND THE GNOMES
Signed
Watercolour with pen and ink and crayon
$7^{7/8} \times 9^{3/4}$ inches

105
THIS DESIRABLE PLOT
Inscribed with title and 'A Dream House-Hunter's
Nightmare'
Watercolour with pen and ink
7$\frac{7}{8}$ x 10$\frac{5}{8}$ inches
Illustrated: Cover for *'Thelwell's This Desirable Plot'*;
paperback edition published by Methuen & Co. Ltd., 1982

106
The Bear and Ragged Staff
Signed
Watercolour with pen and ink
$11\frac{1}{8} \times 9\frac{1}{2}$ inches
Sketch for Inn Sign designs
produced for Guinness
calendars and prints, 1974

107
THREE SHEETS IN THE WIND
Signed
Watercolour with pen and ink
8½ x 13¼ inches
Illustrated: Cover for *'Thelwell's Three
Sheets in the Wind, A Manual of Sailing';*
paperback edition published by
Methuen London Ltd., 1982

108
HOW TO DRAW PONIES
Signed and further titled
'All the Secrets Revealed by Thelwell'
Watercolour, bodycolour with pen and ink
7¾ x 8⅝ inches
Design for Book cover

109
OVER THE GARDEN WALL
Signed
Watercolour, bodycolour and pen and ink
7⅞ x 9¾ inches

110
THE FLY FISHERMAN
Signed
Watercolour with pen and ink
and bodycolour
7⅝ x 10⅛ inches

111
THE CAROL SINGERS
Signed
Watercolour with pen and ink
11 x 16 inches
Design for a Royle's Christmas Card

112
THE JOLLY HUNTSMAN
Signed and inscribed with title
in pencil under mount
Watercolour, bodycolour
and pen and ink
8 x 12 inches

113
THE HUNT OBSERVERS
Signed
Watercolour with pen and ink
18⅜ x 13¼ inches

114
A BIRD IN THE HAND
Signed and inscribed with pencil under mount
Watercolour
8 x 12 inches
Design for The Shooting series of Sporting Prints

115
PUNCH COVER:
AUTUMN
NUMBER
Signed
Watercolour,
bodycolour, pen
and ink with
crayon
12 x 10 inches
Illustrated:
Front cover of
Punch,
September 14,
1966

116
PUNCH COVER:
MOTOR NUMBER
Signed
Watercolour,
pen and ink
with crayon
12 x 10 inches
Illustrated:
Front cover of
Punch, October
16, 1968
*'Wrestling with a
pencil',* page 88;
published by
Methuen
London Ltd.,
1986

117
WET DAY AT WOOD CHURCH,
WIRRAL
Signed and inscribed with title
Watercolour with bodycolour
$14^5/_8 \times 21^3/_8$ inches
From a sketch made in 1948 and
illustrated in *Wrestling with a Pencil*,
page 66, published by
Methuen London Ltd., 1986

118
THE FOX IN WINTER
Signed and dated 1982
Oil on board
14 x 18 inches

119
THE EEL-TRAP BRIDGE
Signed and dated 1978
Watercolour and bodycolour
15 x 21¼ inches
Illustrated: *Wrestling with a Pencil*,
page 145; published by
Methuen London Ltd., 1986

120
PENRUIN WATERMILL,
CORNWALL
Signed
Watercolour with pen
and ink and
bodycolour
9 x 12⅛ inches
Illustrated: Book cover
for *A Millstone
Round My Neck*,
by Norman Thelwell,
published by
Eyre Methuen 1981

121
NORFOLK FARMSTEAD
Signed and dated Dec. 1980
Watercolour and bodycolour
9¾ x 14¼ inches

122
HERONS' MEAD POOL
Watercolour with bodycolour
5⅞ x 8⅛ inches
Illustrated: Front cover of Dust Jacket
to 'A Plank Bridge by a Pool',
by Norman Thelwell;
published by Eyre Methuen, 1978

123
HARBRIDGE, HAMPSHIRE
Signed and inscribed with title
and dated 1988
Watercolour
$14^{3}/_{4}$ x $21^{3}/_{8}$ inches

124
BRIDGE OVER THE LAKE,
HERONS MEAD
Signed and dated 1988
Watercolour
$14^{5}/_{8}$ x $21^{3}/_{8}$ inches

125
BRIXHAM TRAWLERS
Signed and dated 1979
Watercolour
15 x 21¼ inches
Illustrated: *'Wrestling with a Pencil',*
page 165, published by
Methuen London Ltd., 1986

126
THE ANGLER'S ARMS
Signed
Watercolour with pen and ink
$10\frac{1}{2} \times 9\frac{5}{8}$ inches
Sketch for Inn Sign designs
produced for Guinness
calendars and prints, 1974

127
THE TIDE MILL AT BEAULIEU, HANTS
Signed and dated 1985
Watercolour
$14^{5}/_{8}$ x $21^{3}/_{8}$ inches

128
MUDEFORD, HAMPSHIRE
Signed and inscribed with title
and dated 1987
Watercolour
$10^{3}/_{4}$ x $14^{3}/_{4}$ inches

129
THE PIERHEAD, LIVERPOOL
Signed and dated 1983
Watercolour
14³/₄ x 21¹/₂ inches
Illustrated: *Wrestling with a Pencil*,
page 59, published by Methuen
London Ltd., 1986

130
FOOT BRIDGE ON THE RIVER TEST
Signed and dated 1985
Watercolour
13⁵/₈ x 20³/₄ inches

131
JASMINE: 'SHE WOULD LIE IN THE GRASS
AND WATCH ME THROUGH AMBER SLITS.'
Signed with initials
Pen and ink
2 x 3 inches
Illustrated: '*A Plank Bridge by a Pool*', page 76,
published by Eyre Methuen Ltd., 1978

132
TROUT RISE
Signed with initials
Pen and ink
$3^7/8$ x $6^1/2$ inches
Illustrated: '*A Plank Bridge by a Pool*', page 43,
published by Methuen & Co. Ltd., 1978

133
THE SHREW
Signed with initials
Pen and ink
1¾ x 2½ inches
Illustrated: '*A Plank Bridge by a Pool*',
page 76,
published by Eyre Methuen Ltd., 1978

134
'HEDGEHOGS SNUFFLE AND GRUNT NOISILY AS THEY
RUMMAGE ABOUT FOR TASTY MORSELS.'
Signed with initials
Pen and ink
1¾ x 2¾ inches
Illustrated: '*A Plank Bridge by a Pool*', page 37,
published by Eyre Methuen Ltd., 1978

135
THE HERON
Signed with initial
Pen and ink
4½ x 3¼ inches
Illustrated: '*A Plank Bridge by a Pool*', page 121,
published by Eyre Methuen Ltd., 1978

136

'…WILD DUCK WOULD SIT MOTIONLESS ON A CLUTCH OF
GREENISH-WHITE EGGS IN THE RANK GRASS BENEATH THE
ALDERS.'
Signed with initials
Pen and ink
3¾ x 5½ inches
Illustrated: *'A Plank Bridge by a Pool'*, page 11,
published by Eyre Methuen Ltd., 1978

137

KINGFISHER, BUZZARD, HERON, TROUT
Signed with initials
Pen and ink
6 x 6 inches
Illustrated: *'A Millstone Round My Neck'*, pages 17, 26, 76, 125,
published by Eyre Methuen Ltd., 1981

138
MALLARD DRAKE FLYING IN
Signed with initials
Pen and ink
4½ x 4½ inches
Illustrated: *'A Plank Bridge by a Pool',* page 35,
Also inset on dust jacket,
published by Eyre Methuen Ltd., 1978

139
DUCK TAIL
Signed with initial
Pen and ink
2 x 3 inches
Illustrated: *'A Plank Bridge by a Pool',* page 144,
published by Eyre Methuen Ltd., 1978

140
THE MILL WHEEL
Signed with initials
Pen and ink
3¾ x 4½ inches
Illustrated: *'A Millstone Round My Neck'*, page 12,
published by Eyre Methuen Ltd., 1981

141
'…DOWN THE STREAM ONE JUNE DAY…'
Signed with initials
Pen and ink
3 x 6¼ inches
Illustrated: *'A Plank Bridge by a Pool'*, page 108,
published by Eyre Methuen Ltd., 1978

142
THE EDGE OF THE DAM AT THE MILL POOL
Signed with initials
Pen and ink
4½ x 6½ inches
Illustrated: *'A Millstone Round My Neck'*, page 122,
published by Eyre Methuen Ltd., 1978

143
THATCHED COTTAGES UNDER REPAIR
AT KING'S SOMBOURNE
Inscribed with title and with pencil
drawing on back
Pen and ink
2½ x 9¼ inches
Illustrated: *'Wrestling with a Pencil'*,
page 114, published by
Methuen London Ltd., 1986

144
PLANK BRIDGE SKETCH
Signed. Inscribed with sketching details
Pencil
7½ x 10 inches

145
YEW TREE FARM,
CONISTON LAKE
Signed and inscribed
with title in pencil
Pencil
6¾ x 9¾ inches
Illustrated: *Wrestling with a
Pencil'*, page 113,
published by
Methuen London Ltd., 1986

146
THE TIDE MILL
AT BEAULIEU, HANTS
Inscribed with title
and sketching details
Pencil
7 x 11¼ inches
Illustrated: *Wrestling with a
Pencil'*, page 137,
and inside of back cover,
published by
Methuen London Ltd., 1986

147
SKETCHBOOK DRAWINGS OF DONKEYS
IN THE NEW FOREST
Signed
Pencil
5 x 8 inches
Illustrated: *'Wrestling with a Pencil',* page 161,
published by Methuen London Ltd., 1986

148
PHEASANTS AND FOX
Signed
Pencil
4½ x 7¼ inches
Illustrated: *'Wrestling with a Pencil',* page 134,
published by Methuen London Ltd., 1986